D1362421

COMMUNICATIONS

The books in the **MORE SCIENCE IN ACTION** series are

FORCES OF NATURE

HABITATS AND ENVIRONMENTS

MIND AND PERCEPTION

EARTH AND SPACE

CALCULATION AND CHANCE

COMMUNICATIONS

MORE SCIENCE IN ACTION

The Marshall Cavendish Guide to Projects and Experiments

COMMUNICATIONS

Compiled and created by Laura Buller and Ron Taylor
Illustrations by John Hutchinson and Stan North

Marshall Cavendish Corporation · New York · London · Toronto · Sydney

EDITORIAL STAFF

Series Editor	Laura Buller	**Production Controller**	Deborah Cracknell
Assistant Editors	Theresa Donaghey	**Production Secretary**	Jayne Hough
	Caroline Macy	**Managing Editor**	Sue Lyon
Art Editor	Keith Vollans	**Publishing Director**	Reg Wright

Reference Edition published 1990

Published by Marshall Cavendish
Corporation
147 West Merrick Road
Freeport, Long Island
N.Y. 11520

Typeset by Quadraset Ltd.
Printed in Spain

All rights reserved. No part of this book
may be reproduced or utilized in any form
or by any means electronic or mechanical
including photocopying, recording, or by
an information storage and retrieval system,
and without permission from the copyright
holder.

© Marshall Cavendish Limited MCMXC

**Library of Congress Cataloging-in-
Publication Data**

Communications.
   p.   cm. — (More science in action)
   Includes index.
   Summary: Presents projects and
experiments exploring such forms of
communication as ink, television,
photography, heliography, semaphore,
and sound recording.
   ISBN 1-85435-313-6
   1. Telecommunication—Experiments—
Juvenile literature. [1. Communication—
Experiments. 2. Experiments.] I. Marshall
Cavendish Corporation. II. Series.
TK5102.4.C66   1990
621.382—dc20   90-2049
ISBN 1-85435-307-1 (set)   CIP
ISBN 1-85435-313-6 (vol)   AC

CONTENTS

Projects marked ⊕ need adult supervision.

✓91-641

INTRODUCTION

This book will help you learn more about science and technology. It includes experiments, projects, puzzles, and even some tricks. Some of the experiments and projects are very easy. Others are a little harder (they are marked ✢) and you will need help from one of your teachers or parents. You do not have to begin on page 8 — look through the book and start with something you like — but remember that good scientists

- make a record of their work
- have a clean and tidy laboratory
- most important, keep themselves safe (always read pages 40 to 42 before you begin).

EASY PROJECTS

Communications enable people to share and exchange information and ideas. Advances in science and technology have revolutionized communications, so that information can reach huge numbers of people in minutes. You can learn more about communications in the easy projects found on the following pages. Try block printing and make your own ink. Learn about light, then make and use a simple camera. Create pictures from lines to understand how a television picture is made, and test the principle of a satellite dish.

THE LAWS OF NORTH CAROLINA (G. S. 14-398) MAKE IT A MISDEMEANOR TO WILLFULLY DAMAGE, DETAIN, ETC. ANY BOOK, DOCUMENT, ETC. DEPOSITED IN A PUBLIC LIBRARY.

Sound

You will need—

large bucket
2 small rocks
wooden table
glass window
metal baking tray
large book
empty tin can
can opener
masking tape
scissors
deflated balloon
rubber band
strong glue
small mirror, about
    ¼ inch square
table lamp

Sound surrounds us every hour of the day, from traffic rushing past to people talking, from the school bell ringing to crickets singing at night. Each sound is produced by vibration, which the brain interprets after it has entered the ear. Sound can travel through air as well as through other mediums, like earth and water. Whales, for instance, communicate by making sounds to each other while under water. Find out more about sound in the following projects.

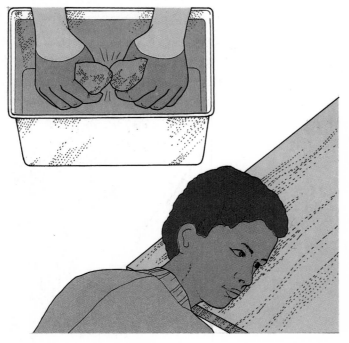

Sound and liquids

Procedure
1. Fill a large **bucket** with water. Hold a **small rock** in each hand, then put your hands into the water in the bucket, making sure the rocks are submerged.
2. Now strike the rocks together sharply. Can you hear any sound?

Sound and solids

Procedure
1. For this experiment, you will need a thick **wooden table** and a friend to assist you. Put your finger into one ear so that you cannot hear anything through it, then put your head down so that your other ear is close to one end of the table as shown.
2. Now ask your friend to scratch the other end of the table with a fingernail. Can you hear anything?
3. Try this experiment with a **glass window**, a **metal baking tray**, and a **book**. What do you discover?

Moving sound

Procedure
1. Ask an adult to remove both ends of an empty, clean **tin can** with a **can opener**. If the edges are still sharp, cover them with **masking tape**.
2. Using **scissors**, cut a **deflated balloon** in half. Stretch the bottom half of the balloon over one end of the can. Hold it in place with a **rubber band**.
3. Use **strong glue** to attach a **small mirror** about ¼ inch square to the outside of the stretched balloon as

shown. It should be about one-third of the way in from the edge of the can.

4. Now stand opposite a dark wall or door. Position the **table lamp** as shown. Then hold the can so that a shaft of light from the table lamp shines onto the piece of mirror and reflects a spot of light onto the wall.

5. Place your mouth at the end of the can opposite the balloon and make noises into it, causing the balloon to vibrate. As you make noises into the can, the mirror and the spot of light reflected onto the wall will move.

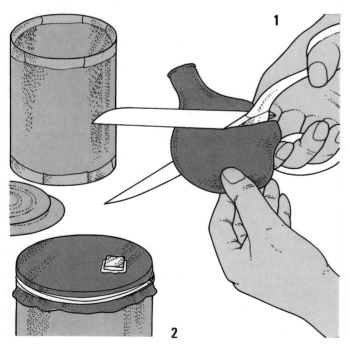

1

2

3

Take care!

A tin can with its top and bottom removed will have sharp, jagged edges. To make it safer, file down the edges at the open ends, or cover them with several layers of tape.

Resonance

You will need—

piano

Resonance is the reinforcing of sound by creating sympathetic and harmonic vibrations in another object. When the clapper of a bell hits the metal surrounding it, for example, the metal will continue to vibrate and resonate for some time afterward. The sound travels in waves through the structure of the bell. A train traveling along the rails causes the rails to vibrate, sending waves ahead of the train. As a result, you can hear the train coming from several miles away if you put your ear down to the ground near the rail.

These examples are the result of a direct impact of one object on another, but resonance is also created by sound itself traveling through the air and causing an object to vibrate without actual contact. You may have seen an opera singer shatter a glass by singing a note with the same frequency as the resonance frequency of the glass. People suffering from kidney stones can be treated with ultrasound waves. These waves break up and disperse the stones, saving the necessity of long surgical operations.

Resonance is used in musical instruments like the flute to increase the loudness of the sound produced by the instrument. Wave patterns fill the column of air inside the instrument; this air column resonates with the vibrations created by the player at the mouthpiece, making the sound of the instrument louder. You can use your voice to create resonance in this project.

Procedure

1. For this experiment, you will only need a **piano** and your voice. Use the piano at school if you do not have one at home. Carefully open the lid of the piano over the strings. At the same time, press down on the right-

hand, or sustain, pedal. (You might need to ask someone else to help you, either by holding the piano lid open or holding down the pedal. Remember to ask them to keep as quiet as possible.) What do you hear when you press down the pedal?

2. Now hum or sing a single loud, clear note into the open top of the piano, still holding down the sustain pedal. Stop singing suddenly and listen closely. What note comes back to you from the piano?

3. Repeat the experiment, but his time check which string or strings resonate with your voice. You can also try making other sounds into the piano. What conclusions can you draw?

Making music

When you play a tune on a musical instrument, you have to make different notes. If the instrument is a stringed one, then you change the notes by pressing the strings with the fingers of one hand while the other hand plucks or bows the strings to produce the sound. The following experiments will show you about the sound of music.

Procedure

1. For the first experiment, you will need a **wooden ruler** and a **heavy book**. Put the ruler with most of its length overhanging on the edge of the table as shown. Put the book on top of the part of the ruler which rests on the table. Hold it down firmly.

2. With your other hand, push down the end of the ruler which is overhanging the table and let it go quickly. It will make a low, twanging sound.

3. Push the ruler back, farther onto the table, still holding it down under the book, so that a shorter length overhangs the table. Pull the ruler down, quickly let it go, and listen. The noise will be much higher in pitch.

4. Repeat the experiment, changing the length of the ruler overhanging the table each time.

5. Use the ruler again in the second experiment. Stretch a **rubber band** along the length of the ruler, and push a **pencil** across each end of the ruler under the rubber band as shown.

6. With a finger, pluck the rubber band in the section between the pencils and listen to the note. Push one of the pencils a little farther along the ruler and pluck the band again. It will make a higher note. By moving one pencil up and down the ruler, you can play a tune.

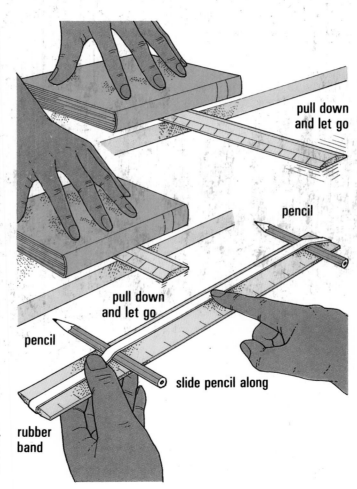

pull down
and let go

pencil

pull down
and let go

pencil

slide pencil along

rubber
band

You will need—

wooden ruler
heavy book
rubber band
2 small pencils

Block printing

You will need—

pencil
2 3-inch square pieces
    of cardboard
scissors
glue
poster paints
paintbrushes
paper towels

Block printing is a method of reproduction by which an image is cut into a thin block of wood or linoleum. Historians believe that the Chinese invented block printing sometime around A.D. 700.

To make a block print, the artist first draws a picture onto a block with a pencil or pen. The lines and areas to be printed are left as they are, but the rest of the block is cut away with special knives called gouges. Then the artist coats the block with thick ink applied with a roller. The ink only covers the raised, uncut parts of the block. Finally, a sheet of paper is pressed onto the block and the image is transferred in reverse to the paper. Try a simple form of block printing in this project.

Procedure
1. Use a **pencil** to draw a simple shape, such as a star, on one of the **cardboard squares**. Cut the shape out carefully with **scissors**, then attach it to the other piece of cardboard with **glue**.
2. When the glue is dry, use a **paintbrush** to paint the entire surface of the shape with **poster paint**.
3. Immediately press the shape firmly, painted side down, onto the paper you want to decorate. Carefully lift the shape away after a few seconds and dry it off with **paper towels**.
4. Now paint the shape with a different color and repeat the printing process.

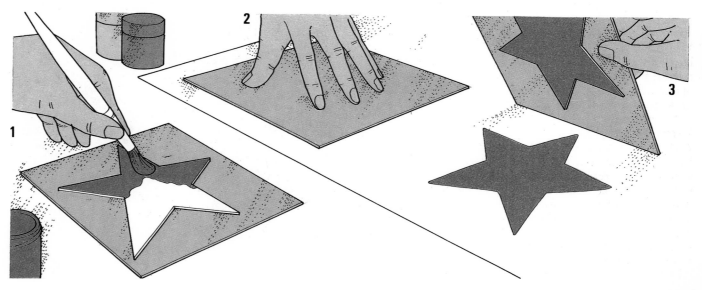

Making ink

Historians believe that ink was used by the ancient Chinese and Egyptians as far back as 2500 B.C. It was made from natural ingredients like berries, bark, soot, and oil. In areas with deciduous forests, the gall from an oak tree was widely used to make ink.

Today, most inks are made from synthetic chemicals which are produced to suit particular requirements. Ball-point pens, for example, need a thick, sticky ink which will not leak out from the small rotating ball which transfers the ink from pen to paper. In a fountain pen, the ink used must be fluid so that it flows easily through the system of tubes leading from the reservoir of ink to the nib, which does the writing. Fountain pen ink contains a mixture of iron compounds and tannic acid to make it fluid.

Ink contains dyes and resins mixed with a solvent. When you have written in ink, the solvent dries, leaving the color on the page. Sometimes, fluorescent materials are added to ink so that it appears more brilliant and, in some cases, glows in the dark. Try making your own ink in this project.

Procedure

1. To make your own ink, you will need two basic ingredients: ferrous sulfate and tannic acid. If these ingredients are not available, you can make your own. To make a ferrous sulfate solution, you need a few **iron nails**, **carbon tetrachloride** (a cleaning solvent), and some **white vinegar**. Put the nails in a **glass jar** and cover them with carbon tetrachloride to remove all traces of grease. Then drain away the fluid and put the nails in a **china cup**. Cover them with about ½ cup of white vinegar, and leave for 48 hours.

2. To make a tannic acid solution, pour ½ cup of water into a **saucepan** and add three tablespoons of **loose Indian tea leaves**. Bring to a boil and allow to boil for several minutes. Then remove the saucepan from the heat and allow the mixture to cool completely.

3. Drain the liquid from the nails and mix with an equal amount of liquid from the tea leaves in a glass jar.

4. If your ink looks too thin to write with, mix in a small amount of **white school glue**, a little at a time.

5. Now fill an old **fountain pen** with your homemade ink. Write a letter with it and note the color of the writing. Leave your letter to stand for 24 hours and check the color of the writing again.

You will need—

10–12 iron nails
carbon tetrachloride
½ cup white vinegar
2 glass jars
china cup
saucepan
loose Indian tea leaves
white school glue
fountain pen and paper

Take care!

When discarding the carbon tetrachloride, make sure that you flush it down the sink with plenty of water. Keep your homemade ink in a clearly labeled jar, away from young children and pets.

Light tricks

You will need—

small, clear glass
    tumbler
2 small coins
square glass or clear
    plastic container
1 teaspoon milk
large sheet of white
    paper
thick book
flashlight
round glass or clear
    plastic bowl

Reflection is the return of a wave of energy, such as light, heat, sound, or radio, after it strikes a surface. Reflected light, for example, bounces back off a smooth surface just like a rubber ball bounces back when thrown at a wall. You can study the way water reflects light in these two projects.

Have you ever looked directly into a pool of clear, still water? You might have been surprised to see your own face reflected in the pool. The smooth surface of the water acts just like a mirror. In fact, before people learned how to make mirrors, they filled bowls with water and looked into them when they wanted to see their own faces. If you were able to look upward from the bottom of a bowl of water, the mirror effect would be the same. Study reflection in these projects.

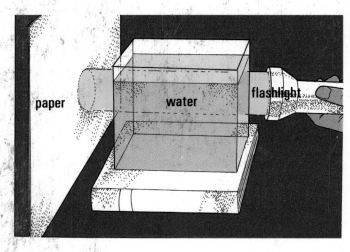

Count the coins

Procedure
1. You will need a small, clear **glass tumbler** and a **small coin**. Pour about an inch of water into the glass.
2. Let the coin fall to the bottom of the glass. Then hold the glass up before your eyes. Keep the glass as steady as you can. You will be able to see two coins, a large one on the bottom of the glass and a smaller one appearing to float just above it. The smaller coin you see is the reflection from the surface of the water of the actual coin, which is lying on the bottom of the glass.
3. Now put the glass down on a table and look into it from above. You will only see one coin. Look at the glass from the side. What do you see then? Try using two coins. How many coins do you see?

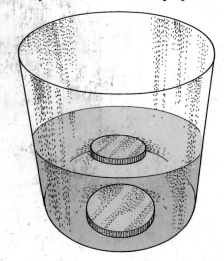

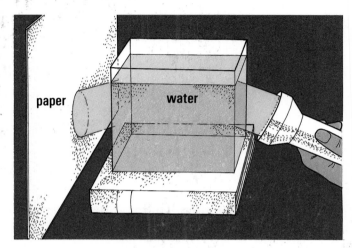

paper

water

Bounce the beam

Procedure

1. You will need a **square glass or clear plastic container** filled with water, one teaspoon of **milk**, a large sheet of **white paper**, a **book**, and a **flashlight**.

2. Stand the square container carefully on the book, making sure not to spill any of the water. Prop up the sheet of paper in front of one end as shown.

3. Next pull the curtains shut or turn out the lights in the room you have chosen to conduct the experiment in so that the room is in darkness. Then turn on the flashlight and shine it through the container as shown. Note the position of the beam on the piece of paper.

4. Now shine the flashlight at an angle through the water as shown. Note where the beam of light is re-

flected on the paper this time. The beam will come out of the container at an angle. This is because when the beam of light from the flashlight hits the top of the surface water, it is bounced back at an angle, whereas if the light is shone straight through the water, it will emerge on the other side in a straight line.

5. Continue your experiment by adding a teaspoon of milk to the water in your container. Now try shining the flashlight through the milky water. See where the beam emerges on the paper at the other side. Shine the flashlight at several different angles, noting each time where the beam emerges.

6. Try the experiment again, but this time use a **round bowl** of water. The square bowl keeps the angles of the beam straight, but a round bowl will distort them.

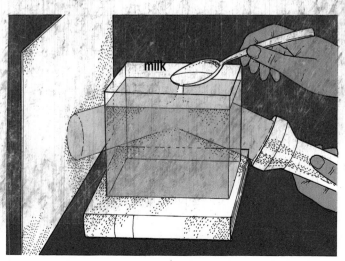

milk

Make a camera

You will need—

cardboard box from a
   roll of 35mm film
aluminum foil
scissors
cellophane tape
needle or pin
black poster paint
paintbrush
small piece of black-
   and-white film
light-tight container
blanket, if needed

The simplest form of camera is a box which is completely free of light inside. At one end of the box is a hole covered by a movable shutter. At the other end is a piece of light-sensitive film. To use this simple camera, the hole is kept covered until you want to take a photograph. Then, the shutter is pointed toward the object you wish to record, and the hole is uncovered so that light can enter the camera and fall on the film inside. Once the film is processed, a negative image is produced from which photographs can be printed.

The trouble with this simple, pinhole camera is that its tiny opening lets in so little light that very long exposures are needed to produce an image on the film contained within it. If the hole is made bigger, the picture it makes becomes much less sharp. This is because the greater number of light rays entering the camera spread over the film, creating an unclear image. Try making and using a simple camera in this project, and see if you can obtain a good picture.

You will need a small section of undeveloped black-and-white film, with a moderately fast ASA rating. You will only need a little piece of film, so it is most economical to ask an adult who takes and develops his or her own black-and-white photos to cut off a few inches of film for you in the darkroom. Then ask him or her to put the film in a completely light-tight box. In addition, you will need to ask him or her to develop, process, and print the film for you when you have completed your experiment. If your school is lucky enough to offer photography classes, ask the photography teacher to help. Finally, you should keep in mind that it is best only to attempt to photograph objects that are well-lighted and completely still.

Procedure

1. You will need an empty **cardboard box** that a roll of 35mm film is sold in, a small piece of **aluminum foil**, a pair of **scissors**, clear **cellophane tape**, a small **needle or pin**, some **black poster paint** and a **paintbrush**, and a small piece of undeveloped, moderately fast **black-and-white film** in a **light-tight container**. First, paint the inside of the film box with black poster paint to stop any light reflection inside the box. Allow the paint to dry completely before you continue.

2. Then cut a piece of aluminum foil with scissors to fit over one end of the box, inside the flap as shown. Use small pieces of tape to secure the foil. Then use a needle to prick a tiny hole in the middle of the foil.

3. Take the film box, the black-and-white film in its light-tight container, the scissors, and the tape into a completely dark closet or under a **blanket**.

4. Carefully remove the film from the light-tight box. Cut off a small section with the scissors. Then tape the piece of film to the opposite end of the box from the foil.

5. Close the box and lower the flap to cover the pinhole in the foil before you leave the darkness. It is essential to follow this step so that you obtain good results.

6. Now leave the darkness. Rest your camera on a firm surface, so that it does not move. Carefully point it at some object and lift the flap over the pinhole for one or two seconds, then lower the flap. Do not move the camera while the flap is up.

7. Now take the camera back into the closet or under the blanket. Carefully lift out the piece of film and put it into a light-tight box. Then ask a friend or photography teacher to develop and print the film for you so you can see the results of your experiment.

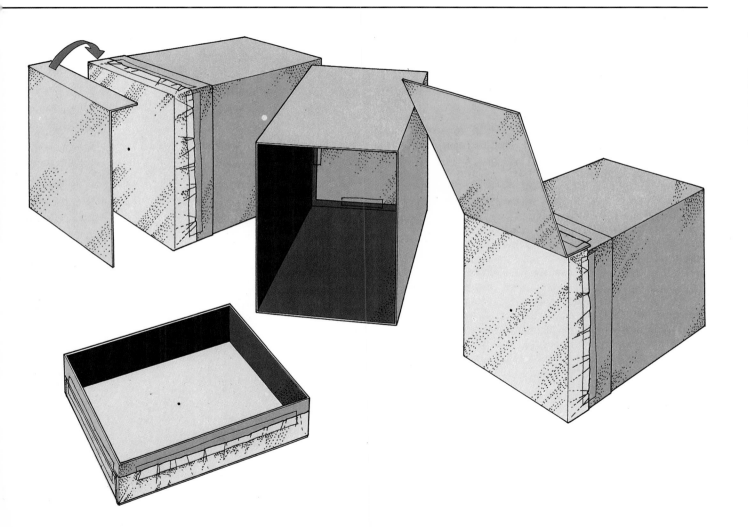

Take care!

Let your eyes adjust to the darkness in the closet for a moment or two before you cut a piece of film to fit your camera.

Newton's disk

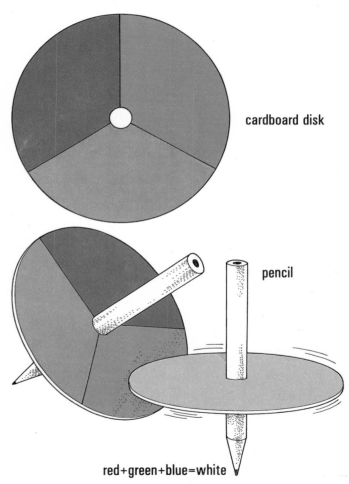

cardboard disk

pencil

red+green+blue=white

You will need—

a sheet of white
cardboard
protractor
scissors
pencil
poster paints
paintbrushes
cellophane tape or
glue

If you mix red and green paint, the result is a muddy brown color. But if you mix red and green light, the result is yellow light. This principle was discovered by the English scientist, Sir Isaac Newton. Newton was a brilliant astronomer and mathematician who also made several spectacular discoveries about light and color around the early 1700s. While experimenting with glass prisms, he found that sunlight shining through a prism came out of the other side split into a rainbow-like band of seven basic colors—red, orange, yellow, green, blue, indigo, and violet. This experiment led Newton to theorize that white light is made up of a mixture of all colors. Test Newton's theory yourself by making the spinning disks in this project.

We know that we can make white light by mixing the seven colors of a rainbow's spectrum. But we can also make white light by mixing just three of the colors—red, green, and blue. These three colors are called the primary colors of light. Color television pictures, for example, are formed by using just these three colors. You will see how the primary colors of light merge to create other colors by spinning your disks. The disk has to spin quite quickly so that the colors appear to blend into a single, new color.

Procedure
1. For this experiment, you will need some thick **white cardboard**, a **protractor**, a pair of **scissors**, a small **pencil**, **poster paints** and **paintbrushes**, and some **cellophane tape or glue**. First, draw a circle about 3 inches in diameter on the cardboard.
2. Using a protractor and a pencil, divide the circle into three equal sections. The angles at the center of the

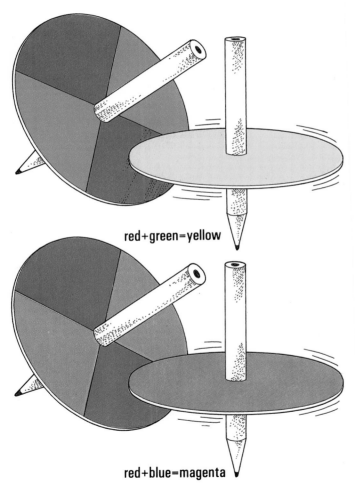

red+green=yellow

red+blue=magenta

disk should all be 120°.

3. Then use poster paint to carefully paint one section red, one section green, and the last section blue. When the paint is completely dry, cut out the disk. Use the point of the scissors to make a small hole in the center of the disk. Push a pencil through the hole, and use either glue or cellophane tape to keep it in position.

4. Spin the pencil to make the disk spin like a top. Watch how the light reflected from the three colored sections appears to blend together. The disk appears to be a smudged white color.

5. Now cut out another cardboard disk. This time, divide it into four equal sections by drawing lines at right angles to each other through the center of the disk. Paint the sectors alternately red and green. Take the pencil out of the first disk and attach it to the second disk in the same way. When you spin the red and green disk, you should be able to see yellow.

6. Repeat the experiment using another four-sectioned disk with the sections painted alternately red and blue. When you spin these colors, a reddish purple color called magenta will appear.

7. Continue to experiment with the colors red, green, and blue on your spinning disks and see what results you find. Try making a disk with two large red sections and two small green sections. The colors should combine to show orange (the shade of orange you get depends on the proportions of red and green you used).

8. Finally, paint a disk with equal sections of red, blue, green, and another red. The double amount of red paint will produce a pinky color, made from the white you produced on the very first disk mixed with the extra red.

Flick book

You will need—

small notebook
pencil
felt-tipped pens or
    colored pencils

During the late 1800s, scientists explained the physiological fact that the brain retains the images of the eye for an instant longer than the eye actually records them. This slow-to-fade effect of human sight is called persistence of vision.

A number of mechanical toys which exploited this optical illusion were invented, with such strange and elaborate names as the Zoetrope, the Stroboscope, and the Praxinscope. These toys usually consisted of a spinning device with pictures drawn upon it, each one showing a different stage of movement.

The effect of persistence of vision is used today in motion pictures and television. Try making this flick book to see how persistence of vision works.

Procedure

1. You will need a small **notebook**. If you do not have a notebook, you could use about 50 sheets of scrap paper stapled together on the left-hand side.

2. Starting at the back of the book, draw a person or animal in the bottom right-hand corner of each page. As you work through to the front of the book, slightly change the position of the arms and the legs to show movement. You might want to use a **pencil** so that any mistakes are easy to erase. When you have made all the drawings in pencil, you can go back over them with **felt-tipped pens** or **colored pencils**.

3. When your drawings are complete, flick through the book from the back to the front.

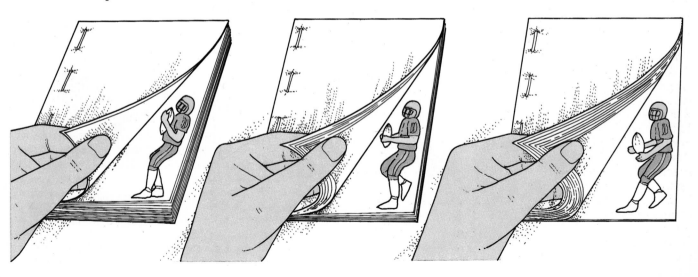

Pictures from lines

The pictures which a television screen displays are actually a type of optical illusion. A television picture is really a tiny spot of light flashing very rapidly across the screen, line by line, over and over again. In the United States, there are 525 lines on each screen. It takes only about 52 millionths of a second to flash, or scan, along one line. This is too fast for human sight to notice. Any image or picture that the human brain receives through the eyes takes about one-tenth of a second to fade, so every part of the television screen seems to be lit up, and the picture always appears to fill the screen.

The brightness of the spot of light varies. It is dim in the dark areas of the picture and bright in lighter areas. You may like to try making your own pictures of lines, divided into dark and light areas, to understand how this effect works on your television set.

Procedure
1. Make your own picture of lines. First, use **tracing paper** and a **pencil** to trace the pattern on the right (you could make a photocopy if you prefer).
2. Fill the pattern following these rules. Start at the top left-hand corner of the "screen" and work your way across and downward. Always work from left to right. Always start each line by shading in black. When you reach an upright mark, stop shading. Start shading again after the next upright mark.
3. Shade and then stop shading until each line is complete. When you have finished, turn the picture upside-down and look at it from a distance with half-closed eyes. What do you see? Try inventing your own picture from lines on a sheet of lined paper.

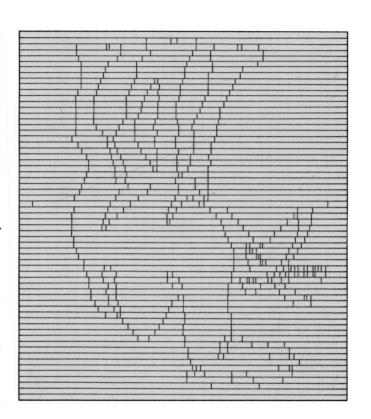

You will need—

tracing paper
pencil

Umbrella antenna

You will need—

2 umbrellas
aluminum foil
masking tape
ticking watch

Satellite communications systems are used to send telephone calls, television signals, and computer data all around the world.

Information is beamed up to the satellite orbiting in space by large dish-shaped transmitters called earth stations. The message travels in the form of microwaves. The satellite gathers up the information with a small dish antenna of its own, boosts the signals, then sends the transmission back to Earth in a wide beam called the satellite's footprint. The receiving antenna has to be dish-shaped to collect this wide signal. The microwaves strike the inside of the dish and are reflected inward so that they all meet at a focus point in the center of the dish. Test this principle by making an umbrella antenna in the following project.

Procedure
1. First open two **umbrellas** and line the insides with **aluminum foil**. Use **masking tape** to secure the foil.
2. Now ask a friend to hold one of the lined umbrellas. Stand a few feet away from each other and point the handles of the umbrellas at one another.
3. Now ask your friend to hold a **ticking watch** near one umbrella while you listen near the other. The sound beam will be picked up and relayed so that the ticking is clearly heard.

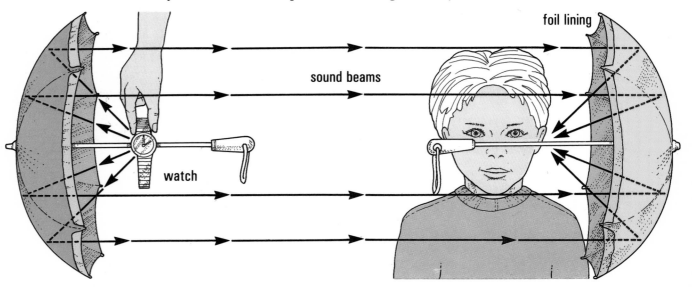

foil lining

sound beams

watch

MORE DIFFICULT PROJECTS

Continue your study of communications with the more difficult projects found on the following pages. You can find out how to send messages with a heliograph, then make your own semaphore flags. Build and test an electric buzzer, or try making a light fader. Study non-verbal communications with a lie detector. Learn how to make good sound recordings and test your skills by recording sound effects. Experiment with photography in the darkroom by making photograms. Construct a pantograph to enlarge and reduce drawings.

Heliography ⚘

2 small, square mirrors
backing blocks to fit the
    mirrors
strong adhesive
perforated metal strips
screwdriver
6 small screws
block of scrap wood
2 narrow softwood strips
balsa wood
craft knife
cutting mat
ruler
pencil
4 wood screws
4 thumbtacks
2 small rubber bands

The heliograph is an instrument designed to send messages by reflecting sunlight with a mirror or pair of mirrors. In the 1800s, heliography became one of the most common means of communication between army units on the battlefield.

The short and long flashes of light used by the heliograph represented the dots and dashes of the Morse code system. Try sending messages on your own heliograph in this project; a Morse alphabet and numeral chart is included on the left to help you.

Procedure

1. The construction of this heliograph is quite difficult, so ask an adult to read through the instructions with you, and make sure you understand them before you begin. You will need two small, square **mirrors**. Ask an adult to cut **backing blocks** from softwood scraps to fit each of the mirrors. Then use a **strong adhesive** to glue the mirrors to the backing blocks.

2. You will need **perforated metal strips** to make the brackets. One strip should be about twice as long as the other. Bend the strips into U-shapes as shown, then use a **screwdriver** and **four small screws** to attach the brackets to the mirrors.

3. Find a **block of scrap wood** to serve as your baseboard. Use a screwdriver and two small screws to secure the brackets to the baseboard as shown. Then ask an adult to cut **two narrow strips** from softwood scraps as shown. Screw these strips to the front of the baseboard to support the shutter mechanism.

4. Construct the shutter mechanism from two pieces of **balsa wood**. Cut each piece of balsa wood to the same width as the baseboard and the same height as the

wooden strips, using a **craft knife** and a **cutting mat**. Then use a **ruler** and **pencil** to mark each piece of balsa wood with three large, identical slots. These slots should be the same size as the bars between them. Then cut the slots you have drawn out carefully with a craft knife and a cutting mat.

5. Mark and cut four small vertical slots in one part of the shutter. This part will serve as the moving front of the shutter mechanism. Now find **four wood screws** with screw heads a little larger than the width of the vertical slots. Pass the screws through the slots, and screw them through the back of the shutter and the two wooden strips as shown. The screws must be loose enough to allow the shutter front to slide smoothly up and down. Position the screws so that in the "up" position, the front piece of the shutter obscures the large slots behind. In the "down" position, these slots should be fully exposed.

6. Next, fasten **four thumbtacks** and **two small rubber bands** to the shutter mechanism as shown. With this arrangement, the shutter is normally in the "up" position.

7. To operate the heliograph, point it in the direction that you wish to send signals. Let any sunlight coming from the front of the heliograph fall directly on the back mirror. Adjust the angle of the back mirror so that the sunlight is reflected onto the back of the shutter. Then send flashes of light by pressing and releasing the shutter. Use a short flash of light to show a dot and a long flash of light to show a dash. If the sun is behind you, arrange the mirrors so that light is reflected from the front mirror onto the back one, then send messages in the same way.

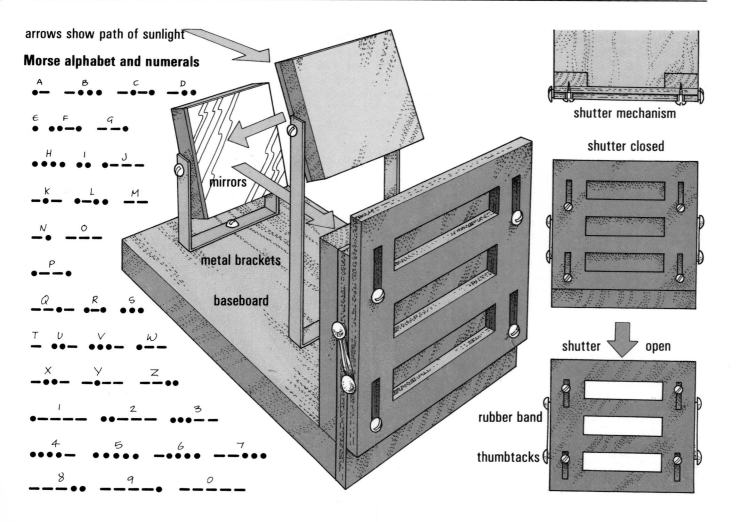

arrows show path of sunlight

Morse alphabet and numerals

A •— B —••• C —•—• D —••

E • F ••—• G ——•

H •••• I •• J •———

K —•— L •—•• M ——

N —• O ———

P •——•

Q ——•— R •—• S •••

T — U ••— V •••— W •——

X —••— Y —•—— Z ——••

1 •———— 2 ••——— 3 •••——

4 ••••— 5 ••••• 6 —•••• 7 ——•••

8 ———•• 9 ————• 0 —————

mirrors

metal brackets

baseboard

shutter mechanism

shutter closed

shutter ⬇ open

rubber band

thumbtacks

Take care!

To cut the slots accurately, it is necessary to use a sharp craft knife. This type of knife can be dangerous and give a nasty cut. So when cutting, use the knife with care, and when you have finished with it, put the safety cover back on.

Semaphore

2 old scarves or
   handkerchiefs, about
   1 foot square
scissors
needle and thread
2 pieces wood dowel,
   about 1½ feet long
pencil
tracing paper

Before the invention of the telegraph, signaling devices such as flags were often used to send messages between distant points. One of the most widely-used methods of flag signaling is called semaphore.

Semaphore was developed by the Frenchman Claude Chappe in 1794. Chappe's system used a set of mechanical arms that pivoted on a post. These arms were mounted on towers spaced between five and ten miles apart. Signal recipients used telescopes to see and "read" the messages.

Today, semaphore signaling is used to send messages between ships at sea or between ships and land. The signaler holds a small flag in each hand and, with arms extended, moves the flags to different angles to indicate letters of the alphabet and numerals from zero to nine. Punctuation is spelled out. Semaphore flags are generally of two colors; red and yellow flags are used between ships at sea, and red and white flags are used between sea and land.

The United States Navy uses semaphore signaling for short-range messages. A person trained in semaphore can both send and interpret messages quickly. On some railroads, mechanical semaphore arms placed on posts along the track give traffic control signals to the train crews.

The most complete flag signaling system is called the international flag code. This system uses more than forty different flags to represent letters and numerals. To send messages, sailors arrange a group of flags called a flag hoist to spell out the message.

You can try sending and receiving semaphore messages with a friend in the following project. With a little practice, you can become quite skilled.

Procedure

1. You and your friend will both need a set of flags and a copy of the signaling chart. First make the flags. You will need two **old scarves** or **handkerchiefs**, each about one foot square, and each in a different color. You could also cut two squares from different colors of fabric scraps, if desired.

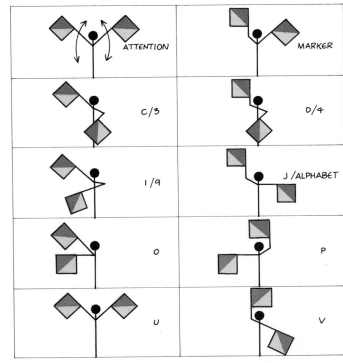

2. Using **scissors**, carefully cut each square of fabric in half on the diagonal. You will now have two triangles of each color.

3. With a **needle and thread**, sew a triangle of one color to a triangle of the other color along the longest edge to give a square shape once again. Then sew together the remaining two triangles. Now tie or sew each of the flags to a piece of **wood dowel**, about 1½ feet long. Make sure the flags are securely attached to the dowels.

4. Now use a **pencil** and **tracing paper** to copy the signaling chart below for your friend (you could make a photocopy instead). Practice sending semaphore messages back and forth with your friend.

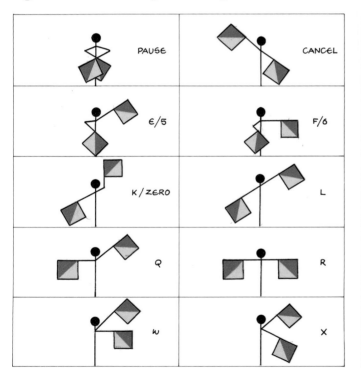

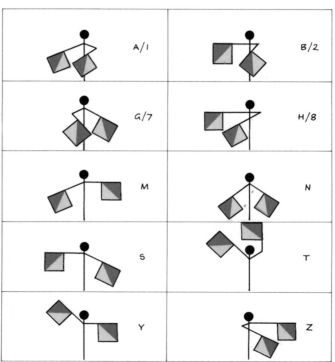

Pantograph ⊡

You will need—

small pencil
thread spool
short section of metal
   pipe
small wooden disk
3 narrow pieces of
   softwood, 16 inches
   long
1 narrow piece of
   softwood, 8 inches
   long
4 bolts, one filed to a
   sharp point
7 nuts
8 metal washers
pointed wooden or
   metal object
paper

The pantograph is a mechanical drawing tool which can copy, reduce, or enlarge an outline drawing quickly and accurately. The pantograph is based on the shape of the parallelogram, a four-sided geometrical figure whose opposite sides and opposite angles are equal. The pantograph works when a tracing point is moved over the design or picture to be copied; another point then moves in unison, copying, reducing, or enlarging the outline. Try making your own pantograph in the following project.

Here are a few guidelines to follow when making your pantograph. Make sure you do not use anything too sharp as a tracer, or you might damage the drawings that you are enlarging or reducing. If you cannot find a suitable tracer, you could try using an old, dried-up ballpoint pen. If you are left-handed, you might find it easier to construct the pantograph so that the pivot is positioned at the end of the 16-inch piece of wood opposite the pencil holder/tracer "arm." You will need to put a rest in the pivot position of the right-handed pantograph shown in the illustrations.

Procedure

1. The pantograph is not difficult to make, but you will need an adult to help you. First, construct the weighted pencil holder. You will need a small, sharpened **pencil**, an empty **thread spool** with a hole big enough to fit the pencil into, a short section of **metal pipe** to provide the weight (you could use a heavy nut if you do not have a suitable section of metal pipe), and a **small wooden disk** to fit inside the pipe to secure everything. Assemble the weighted pencil holder, using the illustration on the right as a guide. Make sure that everything fits together quite tightly.

2. Now make the pantograph frame. You will need **three narrow pieces of softwood 16 inches long**, and **one piece 8 inches long**. You will also need **four bolts**, **seven nuts** to fit the bolts, and **eight metal washers**. In addition, you will need a **pointed wooden or metal object** about the same size as the pencil to serve as your tracer. Ask an adult to study the diagram, then drill holes about ½ inch inside of each corner of all four strips of wood. The holes should be big enough to hold the bolts. You will also need to ask an adult to drill two holes in the exact center of two of the 16-inch pieces of wood as shown. One of these holes will hold the tracer, and the other will hold the pencil in its weighted holder.

3. Assemble the frame, using the diagram as a guide. You will end up with a 16-inch by 8-inch rectangle, with an 8-inch extending "arm." In three of its corners, make a rest as shown, using a bolt with its head pointing downward, two nuts, and two washers. In the other corner, make a pivot. Ask an adult to sharpen the end of the remaining bolt with a file. With the pointed end downward, assemble the pivot, using one nut and the remaining two washers. Insert the tracer into the hole in the extending arm. Insert the pencil with its weighted holder into the final hole. Your pantograph is now ready to use.

4. First try using the pantograph to copy a drawing to half its original size. Try drawing a half-size map of the United States, for example. Find the drawing you want to reduce in a book or atlas. The pencil and the tracer should be in the position shown. Then put a **sheet of**

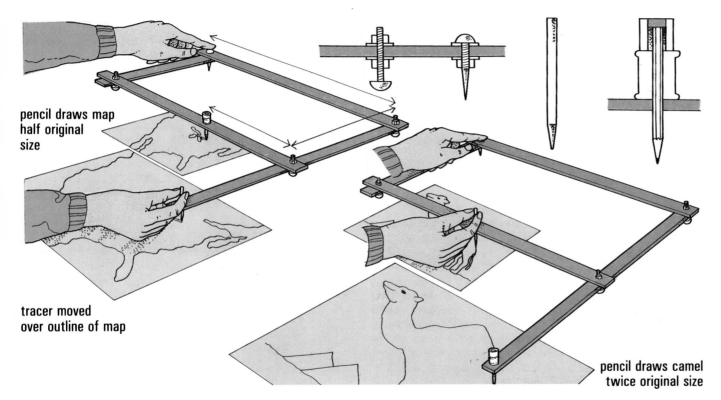

pencil draws map
half original
size

tracer moved
over outline of map

pencil draws camel
twice original size

Be very careful of
the sharp point of the
pivot. Do not use your
pantograph on a
wooden table, where
the pivot could scratch
and damage it.

paper under the pencil. Press down lightly but firmly on the pivot with one hand so that the pantograph does not slide while you are making the copy. Use your other hand to guide the tracer over the outline of the map.

5. Now try using the pantograph to copy a drawing to twice its original size. You could try drawing the

outline of an animal such as a camel. Find the drawing you want to enlarge in a book. Exchange the positions of the tracer and the weighted pencil. Put a large sheet of paper under the pencil. Now, holding the pantograph lightly but firmly at the pivot as before, move the tracer over the outline of the camel.

Electric buzzer ⊸⊏⊐⊸

You will need—

1 razor blade, blunted
  by an adult
push-button switch
6 or 9-volt dry battery
3 angled steel brackets
3 small screws
block of wood
2 medium-sized screws
long screw
thin enameled or
  plastic-coated wire
wire cutters

At your house or apartment, you probably have an electric buzzer or doorbell fitted near the front door. The button at the door is connected to an electric circuit. When the button is pressed, current flows through an electromagnet. The charged electromagnet causes a moving part called the armature to vibrate, striking a plate or bell to create sound. The buzzer will continue to sound as long as someone is pressing the button. Try this project to find out more about how an electric buzzer works.

Procedure

1. Assemble all the materials you will need to make the electric buzzer. It is very important that you ask an adult to blunt the **razor blade** for you before you begin, so that you do not hurt yourself when handling it. You will also need a **push-button switch** (available at electrical supply stores), a **6- or 9-volt dry battery**, three **angled steel brackets** as shown, three **small screws** to hold the brackets to a **block of wood**, two **medium-sized screws**, one **long screw**, thin **enameled or plastic-coated wire**, and **wire cutters**. First, ask an adult to help you attach the brackets to the wooden base in the positions shown, using three small screws.

2. Now ask an adult to help you attach the blunted razor blade to one of the pair of brackets. Attach it quite firmly to one screw; it should only just touch the other screw. Be very careful when handling the blade.

3. Leaving two long ends, wrap a tight coil of wire around and around the long screw as shown. Then put the wrapped screw into the third bracket as shown.

4. Strip the coating from the long ends of the wire.

Attach one end of the wire to a connection on the push-button switch. Attach the other long end to the screw which is firmly holding the blunted razor blade.

5. To complete the wiring, use wire cutters to cut a length of wire to fit from the press button switch to the negative terminal of the battery. Strip the ends of the wire and attach as before. Then cut a length of wire to fit from the small screw just touching the blunted razor blade to the positive terminal of the battery. Strip the

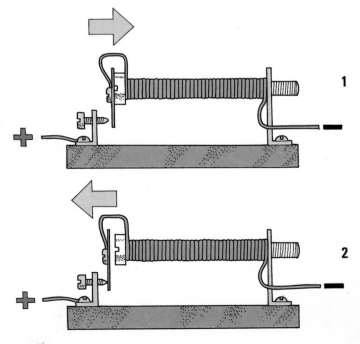

ends and attach as before.

6. Your electric buzzer is now complete. Here is how it works: when the switch button is pressed, the electric circuit is completed, allowing electricity to flow through the wire from one terminal of the battery to the other. The small contact screw, with its point just touching the razor blade, is part of this circuit (see illustration 1). As the current flows through the wire coiled around the long screw, the long screw becomes an electromagnet. The electromagnet pulls the razor blade away from the contact screw (see illustration 2). This action serves to break the circuit; no electricity flows through the coil, so the electromagnet loses its energy. The razor blade springs back to make contact with the screw, completing the circuit again and re-energizing the electromagnet. The process is repeated over and over again. As the razor blade springs back and forth it makes a buzzing sound.

Take care!

It is essential that the razor blade is blunted by an adult before you begin. Be very cautious when handling the blade.

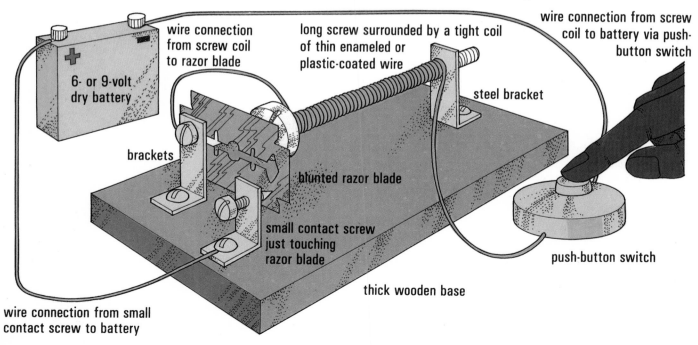

wire connection from screw coil to razor blade

long screw surrounded by a tight coil of thin enameled or plastic-coated wire

wire connection from screw coil to battery via push-button switch

6- or 9-volt dry battery

steel bracket

brackets

blunted razor blade

small contact screw just touching razor blade

push-button switch

thick wooden base

wire connection from small contact screw to battery

Light fader ⚙

You will need—

6-volt battery
3½-volt flashlight bulb in
    a bulb holder
6 feet of thin enameled
    or plastic-coated wire
wire clippers or scissors
aluminum foil
2 paper clips
cellophane tape
glass
few tablespoons salt
spoon

If you have a toy theater or a dollhouse, you can make this simple light fader to use in it. A salt solution is used in the light fader as an electric conductor.

In 1729, the English scientist Stephen Gray found that some substances conduct, or transmit, electricity but others do not. Substances are described as being good conductors when they contain charged particles that are free to move. Some metals, like copper and silver, are very good electric conductors. But liquids can serve as conductors, too. Table salt, for example, is made of sodium and chloride ions. When table salt is dissolved in water, these ions separate and are free to move. If an electromotive force (or voltage) is passed through the salt water solution, the chloride ions move in one direction and the sodium ions move in the opposite direction. The flow of these ions generates a current.

You can test the conductivity of a salt water solution in the following project. Be sure that you read the directions completely before you begin. If you do decide to use your light fader in a toy theater or dollhouse, make sure you disconnect the wires from the battery terminals and discard the salt solution when you have finished using the light fader.

Procedure

1. The current used in this project is not strong enough to hurt you, but you should ask an adult to help you with this project because there are so many steps to follow. First assemble the materials you will need to make your light fader. From an electrical supply store, you will need to buy one **6-volt battery**, one 3½-volt bulb, a **bulb holder** to fit the bulb, and six feet of

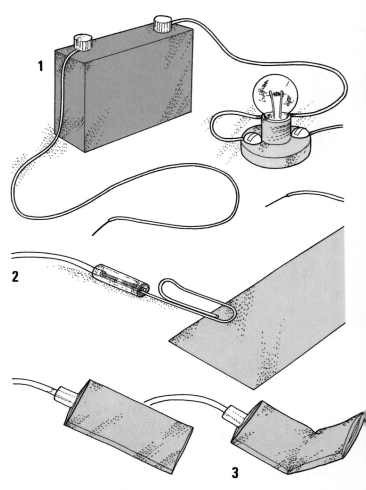

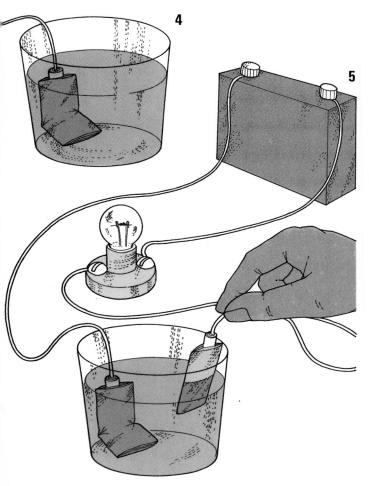

4

5

thin electrical wire with a plastic coating.

2. Use **wire clippers** or an old pair of **scissors** to cut the wire into two 14-inch long pieces and one 1-yard long piece. Then strip about an inch of the plastic covering from each end of all three pieces of wire. You might try nicking the wire with scissors first, then using your fingernails to pull off the plastic covering.

3. Attach one short length of wire to each contact (positive and negative) on the battery. Then carefully screw the bulb into the bulb holder.

4. Attach the other end of one wire to one screw of the bulb holder. Then attach the long piece of wire to the other screw of the bulb holder.

5. Now make terminals, or the ends of the electric circuit. You will need two small pieces of **aluminum foil**, two **paper clips**, and **cellophane tape**. Open out both paper clips to the shape shown. Then use tape to attach an opened-out paper clip to each of the two spare ends of wire.

6. Fold a piece of aluminum foil around each paper clip to make a neat package as shown. Now bend the spare aluminum foil into a U-shape.

7. Make the salt water solution. Fill a **glass** with water. Add a tablespoon of **salt** and stir with a **spoon** until the salt dissolves completely. Keep adding salt and stirring well until no more salt will dissolve.

8. Put one aluminum foil terminal into the glass of salt solution, bending the wire as shown so that the foil terminal sits at the bottom of the glass.

9. Put the other terminal into the glass of salt solution in the same way. The bulb will get brighter as the terminals come closer together, and dimmer as they come further apart.

Sound recording

You will need—

cassette recorder and
  blank cassette tape
a few of the following:
  winter coat, blanket,
  large piece of felt,
  pillow, styrofoam
  packaging,
  cardboard boxes,
  corrugated paper,
  ceiling tiles
notebook and pencil
uncooked rice
piece of wood
funnel
cellophane
a few twigs
small section of an old
  basket
box of wooden matches
wooden or metal box
marbles
masking tape

Experiment with recording sound in these projects. You will need a cassette recorder (an inexpensive one is fine) with either a built-in or separate microphone.

In the first project, you will learn how to control reverberation. When a sound wave leaves its source and travels toward a microphone, many things can happen to it along the way. It may fade, be absorbed, or be reflected. In a room with many reflective surfaces, like a tiled bathroom, much of the sound reaching the microphone will have been reflected, reaching the microphone a fraction later in time than the rest of the sound waves. This effect is called reverberation. When recording speech, too much reverberation will make the words indistinct. See how you can control it with sound-absorbing materials in the first project.

Once you have learned how to make good voice recordings, you might want to try recording some sound effects, following the guidelines in the second project.

Controlling reverberation

Procedure

1. A tiled bathroom is a good place to make reverberation, and is therefore a good place to find out how to control it. Gather a few sound-absorbing items (you do not need to use all the items, but it is interesting to try as many as you can): a **winter coat**, a **blanket**, a large piece of **felt**, a **pillow**, some **styrofoam packaging**, a few **cardboard boxes**, a section of **corrugated paper**, and a few **ceiling tiles**. You will also need a **notebook** and **pencil**.

2. Take the **cassette recorder** into the bathroom and record yourself speaking a few sentences. Then, one by

one, bring an item from the list into the room. Make another recording, keeping track of the items you have introduced in your notebook. Listen to the tape you have made. Which items were successful in helping to control reverberation? Make a few more recordings, experimenting with the materials you felt worked best. With a little practice, you can judge how to place items and what items to place in a room in order to make your speech recordings sound good.

Sound effects

Procedure

1. Try recording the following sound effects. To make rain, drop grains of **uncooked rice** on a **piece of wood**. You could pour the rice through a **funnel** to make a steady rainfall sound.

2. The best way to simulate a fire is to crumple a piece of **cellophane** into a ball with your hands, placing them very close to the microphone. Ask a friend to break a few **twigs** at the same time to make the creak of breaking wood.

3. A crash sound can be made by crushing a **small section of an old basket** close to the microphone. You could also try crushing a **box of wooden matches** for a very realistic sound.

4. Try recording a simulated explosion. Fill a **wooden or metal box** with a few **marbles** and secure the lid with **masking tape**. Then slam the box down sharply on a table and rotate it for a few seconds afterward.

5. Perhaps the best way to discover sound effects is to tape an unusual noise whenever you hear it. Then listen back to the noise. What does it sound like to you?

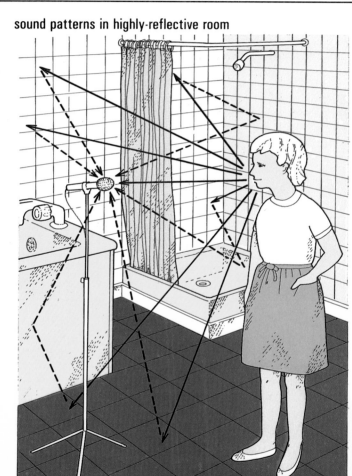

sound patterns in highly-reflective room

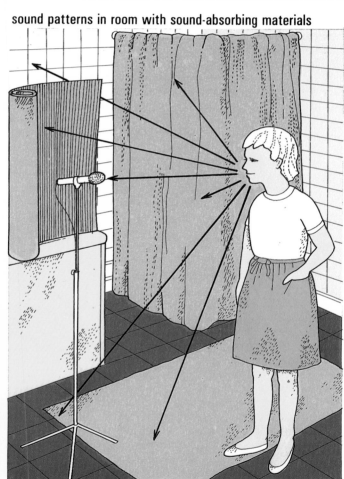

sound patterns in room with sound-absorbing materials

Take care!

As with any electric appliance, do not use the cassette recorder near water.

Lie detector

You will need—

multimeter
2 cans with metal
  press-on lids
2 feet of thin, plastic-
  coated wire
cardboard
scissors
felt-tipped pens or
  colored pencils

If you tell a lie, will your body give you away? You can find out in this project.

A lie detector, or polygraph, is a device that can be used to help decide whether a person is lying. Scientists have found that when a person is asked a question, certain physical changes can occur, depending on the person's emotional reaction. These changes can include alterations in blood pressure, pulse rate, perspiration rate, and breathing rate.

A lie detector is designed to record these physical changes. If a person agrees to take a lie detector test, he or she sits in a chair and answers simple, yes-or-no questions. Pulse rate, blood pressure, breathing rate, and perspiration rate are all monitored throughout the questioning period. The readings are printed out on a moving graph.

When the test is finished, a lie detector examiner looks at the graph. If a person lies, the graph normally shows a change in one or more of the factors. If a person tells the truth, the factors show little or no change.

Although lie detector tests are widely used by the police and other criminal investigators to determine whether a suspect is involved in a particular crime, the accuracy of the tests is a subject of much debate. Polygraph examiners feel the tests are very reliable, but some legal experts are unsure that evidence gathered by a lie detector test is accurate enough to use in court. In most criminal cases, lie detector testimonies are not used as evidence in court.

Try making a simple lie detector. Remember, your lie detector will only measure one of many physical factors associated with lying, so use it for fun rather than accuracy!

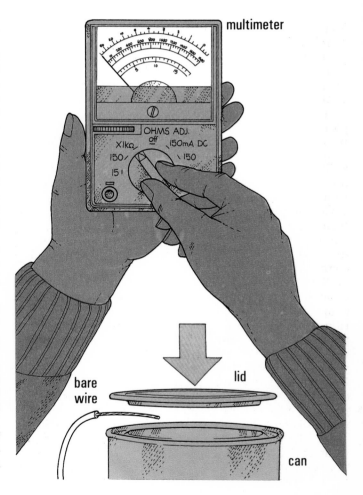

multimeter

bare wire

lid

can

Procedure

1. You will need a **multimeter** (an electrical test meter) for this project. If you do not have one, find out if you can borrow one from a friend, or use the multimeter in your school's science lab. You will also need two **cans with metal press-on lids**, about 2 feet of **thin, plastic-coated wire**, some **cardboard** to make the scale, a pair of **scissors**, and **felt-tipped pens** or **colored pencils**. First, set the multimeter to the resistance range marked Ω×1k (thousands of ohms).

2. Then cut the plastic-coated wire in half to give two one-foot lengths. Strip about an inch of plastic coating from each end of both lengths of wire.

3. Connect one end of one length of wire to the negative terminal on the multimeter and put the other end in one of the cans, using the lid to hold it in place as shown. Repeat with the other length of wire, connecting the positive terminal to the other can.

4. Now make the scale. Cut a circle of cardboard big enough to fit over the multimeter. Then mark a wedge shape on the cardboard as shown. Color it in with felt-tipped pens or colored pencils. Divide the wedge in half with a solid line; label one side "true" and the other side "false." Cut a slot in the wedge as shown so that you can read the multimeter.

5. Now get a friend to place his or her hands on the cans. The meter needle should deflect, showing the person's electric resistance. Position the scale on the multimeter so that the needle is in the middle. Then, the questioning can begin. Remember, if you want to test another person, you will need to re-set the scale to take into account any difference in electric resistance.

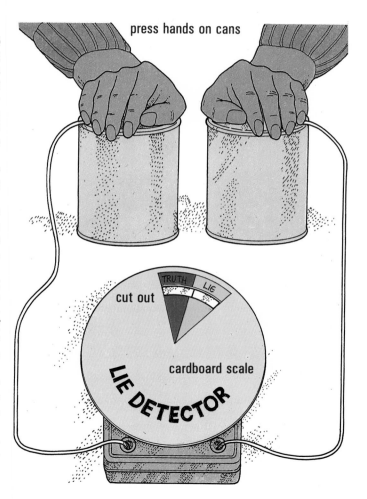

press hands on cans

cut out

TRUTH LIE

cardboard scale

LIE DETECTOR

Photograms ⌖

You will need—

4 darkroom trays
developer
stop bath
fixer
2 pairs of tongs
few sheets of
    photographic paper
    (RC is best)
enlarger and enlarger
    easel
cardboard
selection of objects:
    keys, scissors, paper
    clips, coins, slices of
    fruit

A photogram is the simplest kind of photograph. You do not need a camera to make photograms—simply some photographic paper, a light source, and something to place in the path of the light. Whatever you put in the path of the light casts a shadow on the paper, and the photogram is really the negative image of this shadow. With a little imagination and a few basic darkroom techniques, you can create attractive and unusual photograms in this project.

Photographic paper is coated with an emulsion that contains light-sensitive silver salts. When the paper is exposed to light, chemical changes occur, producing a latent image on the paper that contains all the details that will appear in the final print. The exposed printing paper is put into a flat tray of developer. The chemicals in the developer convert the exposed silver salts on the surface of the paper into metallic silver, forming a visible image. Next the paper is put into a stop bath, which chemically neutralizes the developer. Then the paper is put into the fixer, which helps to

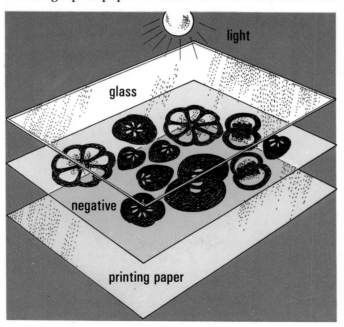

light
glass
negative
printing paper

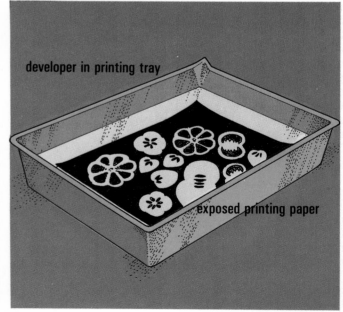

developer in printing tray
exposed printing paper

make the image permanent. After washing and drying, the print is finished.

Procedure

1. Ask an adult with darkroom experience to help you. First set out four **trays**: one each for **developer**, **stop bath**, and **fixer**, and one filled with water to hold the prints after fixing. You will need two **pairs of tongs** (one for the developer and one for the stop bath and fixer). Ask an adult to prepare the solutions for you and put them in the appropriate trays. You will also need a few sheets of **photographic paper** and an **enlarger**. Resin-coated (RC) paper is the best choice.

2. Now make a test print to determine the characteristics of the paper you are using. Turn out the darkroom light (you can leave the safelight on). Put a piece of the photographic paper you are using into the enlarger easel. Stop down the enlarger lens to $f/11$. Cover the paper with **cardboard** except for one narrow strip. Expose this area for 5 seconds, then uncover a second strip, exposing this and the first strip for 5 seconds. Continue to move the cardboard across the paper, making a series of 5-second exposures. Then develop, stop, fix, and wash the print. You will see a range from clean white to solid black on your paper. Work out what exposure time will be best to give the particular tone of gray, black, or white that you want.

3. Now you are ready to make a photogram. With the enlarger lens set at $f/11$, put a piece of paper on the baseboard and place the objects you have chosen on top. Try everyday objects like keys, scissors, paper clips, and coins. You could also try slices of fruit for an interesting effect. Anything that reflects, refracts, or diffuses light

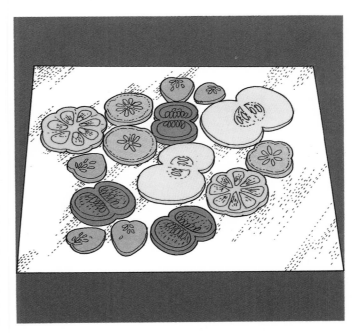

is worth trying. Now make the exposure, using your test print to determine exposure time. Remove the objects after the exposure and process the paper.

4. Take a look at your finished photogram. You will see black paper with white silhouettes of the objects which you placed on the paper. The sharpness of the edges of the objects depends on the height above the paper of the edge that cast the shadow, and the aperture of the enlarger lens. The smaller the aperture, the sharper the edges. Try making a few more photograms.

Take care!

It is important to use tongs so that no chemicals splash onto your skin. If they do, be sure to wash your hands immediately.

SAFETY FIRST!

The safe and simple projects and experiments in this book cover many fields of science and technology, and have been designed to demonstrate and explain important scientific principles in an interesting and straightforward way. Good scientists take care to protect themselves and other people, so always follow these rules for perfect safety.

*FIRE Take care when using matches or candles, and keep a pail of water nearby in case of accidents.

*MAIN LINE ELECTRICITY Use low-power batteries as directed in this book. Do not use the main line—it can kill.

*CHEMICALS Use with care, label clearly, and store out of reach of young children and animals.

*SHARP EDGES Where possible, file edges smooth, and always protect your hands with thick gloves.

And remember . . . before you begin, always get permission from an adult, and if in doubt, ask for help!

SAFETY

The chemicals used in the projects can all be handled safely. Most are common household substances such as salt, baking powder, vinegar, etc.

When a project calls for an electricity supply, there is no danger of electric shock because a low-voltage battery is used.

A few projects involve the use of a flame or heat from a stove. In such cases, younger experimenters should be supervised by an adult, but the procedure is as safe as cooking.

SUPERVISION

The projects have been graded according to the need for adult supervision. Where a project is marked with an ⊕, it means that, for complete safety, an adult should assist the young experimenter with some aspects of the project. In many cases, the adult's assistance will be limited to helping with some parts of the project, such as using a hammer and nails, and then letting the experimenter continue the project with only background supervision. Similarly, it may be necessary for an adult to handle matches or candles.

In other cases, the adult can prepare the materials which are needed for the experiment.

For example, if the project includes accurate cutting out with a sharp knife, the experimenter need not handle the knife if the adult does the cutting out beforehand.

It is a good idea for an adult to be present when the project involves breakable objects like glass jars. A little guidance will minimize the risk of breakages.

SHARP EDGES

Wherever it is possible, the materials chosen for the projects are the safest ones that can be used. Sometimes, there is a choice of materials. For instance, the risk of sharp edges is reduced if you use plastic glass, but if you do use conventional glass, the chance of getting cut will be minimized if you are careful. First, protect your hands with gloves and use a small file or some sandpaper to remove any sharp edges. Handle the glass carefully and never put too much strain on it.

Similar precautions should be taken if the project involves cutting metal. Again, wear gloves and file off any sharp points. For extra safety, cover the cut edges with thick cellophane tape. If the project uses an empty tin can, try to find a can with a push-fit lid. This means you do not need to use a can opener, which will leave a sharp edge.

CHEMICALS

The chemicals used in the projects are all harmless, but they should still be treated with care. Keep each chemical in a labeled jar, and make sure that the jars are stored out of reach of inquisitive small children. Do not experiment with chemicals anywhere near food. Cover the worktable with old newspaper; it will catch any spilt chemicals and can be thrown away later. After the experiment, wash thoroughly the jars or dishes that have been used and pour the old chemicals down the sink, flushing them away with lots of water. Finally, wash your hands thoroughly to remove any traces of chemicals on the skin.

FIRE

You should take extra care with those projects which involve matches or candles. Organize the worktable so that there are no scraps of paper lying around and make sure that you are not wearing loose clothing, such as a tie or scarf, which might accidentally catch fire. Check that you have all the materials needed for the experiment before you begin and arrange them on the worktable so that you do not need to reach over the candle. Always keep a pail of water close at hand just in case there is an accident.

PROCEDURE

Before starting work on a project, it is important to read the instructions through to the end and to form a clear idea of what has to be done, and in what order. Materials and tools needed are listed in the margin and are spelled out in **bold type** when they are first mentioned. Make sure that everything is at hand when it is needed. Many of the projects or experiments can be carried out more smoothly if a little preparatory work, like weighing or cutting out, is done beforehand.

SCIENCE AND THE FUTURE

There are more and more opportunities for scientists in the modern world. Every year, new scientific discoveries help to change the world we live in. Most aspects of our life, including transport, entertainment, medicine, and industry are changing rapidly because of the new inventions and discoveries that scientists are making. When you work on the projects in this book, you will learn many of the basic scientific principles which have helped important scientists to make their contribution to our world. Maybe one day, if you decide to become a scientist, you will join the great men and women of science who will create the world of the future.

WORDS YOU NEED TO KNOW

In this book, you may find some words that you have not seen before. These four pages explain as simply as possible what these words mean and will help you to understand exactly how to do the projects or experiments. Some words are special descriptions invented by scientists, and so are often very complicated to explain — in fact, whole books have been written about them! Of course, there is not enough space in this book to include these very long explanations but if you want to read more, ask your teacher or librarian to help you find a book.

Absorbed
Swallowed up or taken in

Antenna
Wire or rod for TV or radio reception

Aperture
The diameter of the opening in a camera

Armature
The vibrating part in an electric bell

Beam
Ray of light or energy

Circuit
In electricity, the path of a current

Conduct
To transmit electricity

Current
Flow or movement of electricity

Develop
In photography, to make the picture visible

Developer
In photography, chemical solution used to develop exposed film

Distort
To change the usual shape or appearance of

Easel
In photography, a frame to hold printing paper

Electromagnet
Temporary magnet produced by electric current

Emulsion
In photography, a suspension of silver salts in gelatine, used to coat film or plates

Enlarger
Instrument used to project a negative image onto light-sensitive paper

Exposure
In photography, to allow light to fall on light-sensitive material

Fixer
A chemical solution that makes a photographic image insensitive to light

Flag hoist
Group of flags raised together as a signal

Focus point
Point where rays or waves come together

Frequency
A particular wave motion at one special level

Harmonic
Waves superimposed on a fundamental wave, having a frequency which is an exact multiple of the fundamental frequency

Image
Picture or likeness of a thing or person

Interpret
To translate or make understandable

Ions
Electrically charged atoms or group of atoms

Latent image
Image formed by the changes to the silver grains in photographic emulsion upon exposure to light; the image is not visible until chemical development takes place

Medium
A substance through which bodies move

Microphone
Device to change sound waves to electric impulses

Microwaves
Extremely short electro-magnetic waves

Morse code
Telegraphic alphabet made up of a series of dots and dashes

Negative
In photography, an exposed and developed film on which light and shadow are the reverse of the positive printed from it

Neutralize
To make ineffective

Ohms
The unit of electric resistance

Pitch
The quality of sound set by the frequency—the greater the frequency, the higher the pitch

Pivot
A shaft or point on which anything turns

Print
A photograph, especially one made from a negative

Prism
A transparent body used to concentrate and reflect light rays

Reflection
Change of direction when a ray of light or energy strikes a surface and is thrown back

Reinforce
To make stronger

Relay
To receive and pass on a signal

Represent
To stand for; to be a sign for

Resonate
To reinforce and prolong sound waves

Retain
To hold or keep

Reverberation
Multiple reflection of sound waves which prolongs the original sound

Satellite
Man-made object put into orbit around the earth

Scan
In television, to move over rapidly with a beam of light

Shutter
Device for opening and closing the aperture of a camera lens

Silhouette
An outline drawing filled in with a solid color

Solution
Homogenous mixture of
something with water

Solvent
A substance that dissolves
another substance

Stop bath
Acid solution which stops
the action of the developer

Synthetic
Artificial; made by a
chemical process

Tannic acid
Yellowish, astringent
substance

Tone
Vocal or musical sound

Transmitter
Device that generates
radio waves and sends
them through space by
means of an antenna

Unison
Together; in agreement

Vibration
Movement to and fro; to
give off sound by moving

Voltage
The electromotive force of
a supply of electricity,
expressed in volts

Wave
A series of advancing
impulses set up by a
vibration, as in the
transmission of light
or sound

INDEX

UNION COUNTY PUBLIC LIBRARY

816 E. Windsor St.   Monroe. N. C. 28110

J 540.7 MORE/v. 6
*
More science in act><xperiments
MV-J-NON   91-641

8710 92001 51151 7

Books may be borrowed for 3 weeks
Renewals will not be made
OVERDUE books will be charged for
at the rate of 15¢ per day
The library is not responsible
for reminding you. The DATE
CARD in this pocket is your
reminder. Do not remove it

Union County Public Library
Monroe, North Carolina   28110